TOY WORDS

Notes for Parents

Usborne Babies' Library is a new and original approach to books for parents to share with their babies and toddlers. Each page has a clear picture of a familiar object which babies will learn to recognize and relate to real objects and, later, to name.

As they grow older, they will begin to take notice of the little pictures round the edges of the pages. These provide endless opportunities for parent and child to talk about the variety of objects which have the same name, the things that can be done with them and associated objects and events.

Conversations stimulated by looking at these pages will help very young children extend their language and understanding of the things around them.

At a later stage, but long before they learn to read, the words on each page will help children realize that sounds can be written down and that objects can be represented by both pictures and words.

With consultant advice from John Newson and Gillian Hartley of the Child Development Research Unit at Nottingham University, and Robyn Gee.

TOY WORDS

Jenny Tyler
Illustrated by Sue Stitt

Designed by Kim Blundell and Mary Cartwright

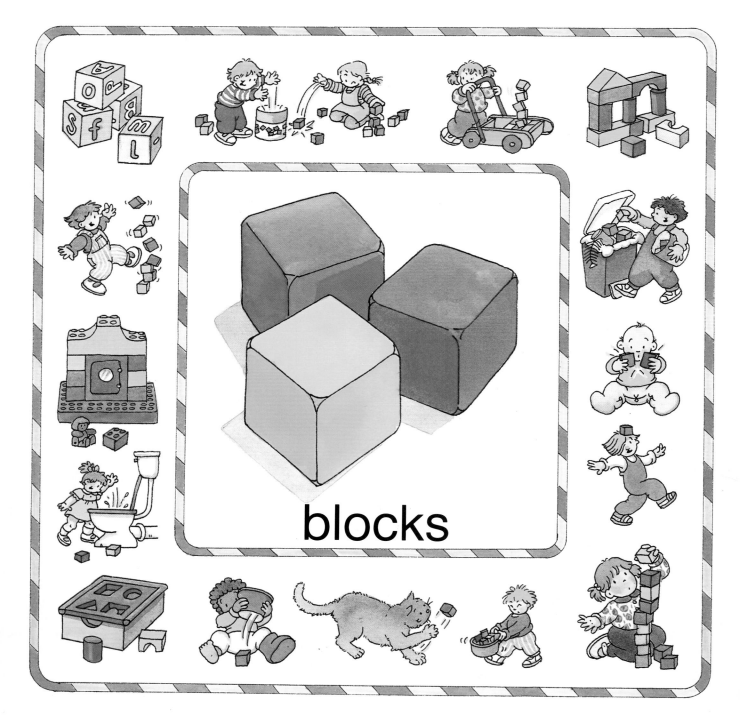

blocks

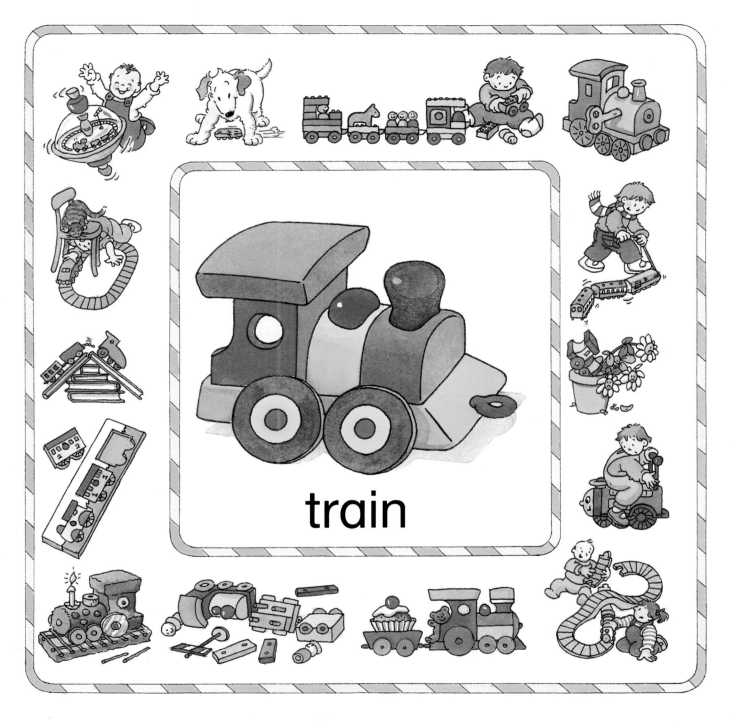

train

car

doll

tractor

airplane

ball

telephone

puzzle

balloon

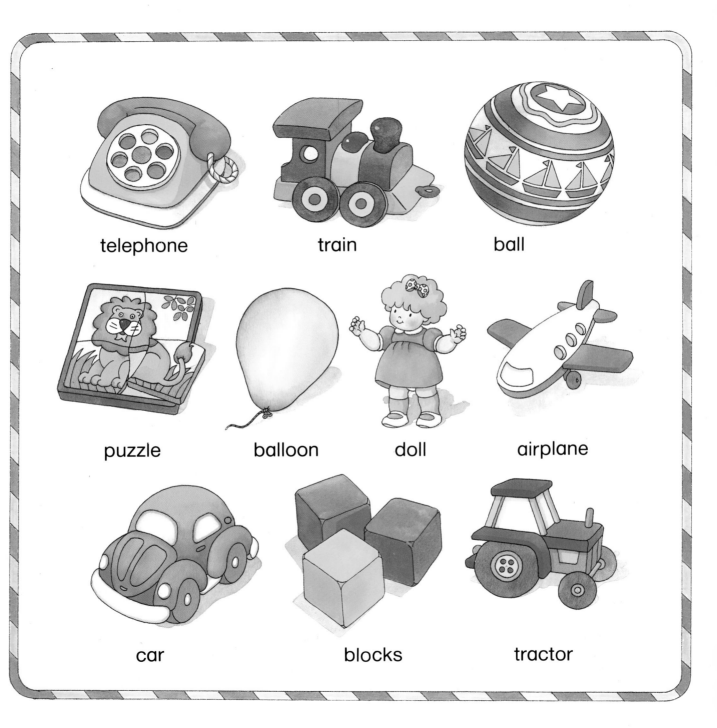

telephone

train

ball

puzzle

balloon

doll

airplane

car

blocks

tractor